Lerner SPORTS

HANK AARON

HOME RUN HAMMER

PERCY LEED

LERNER PUBLICATIONS ◆ MINNEAPOLIS

Copyright © 2022 by Lerner Publishing Group, Inc.

All rights reserved. International copyright secured. No part of this book may be reproduced, stored in a retrieval system, or transmitted in any form or by any means—electronic, mechanical, photocopying, recording, or otherwise—without the prior written permission of Lerner Publishing Group, Inc., except for the inclusion of brief quotations in an acknowledged review.

Lerner Publications Company
An imprint of Lerner Publishing Group, Inc.
241 First Avenue North
Minneapolis, MN 55401 USA

For reading levels and more information, look up this title at www.lernerbooks.com.

Main body text set in Myriad Pro Semibold.
Typeface provided by Adobe.

Library of Congress Cataloging-in-Publication Data

Names: Leed, Percy, 1968– author.
Title: Hank Aaron : home run hammer / Percy Leed.
Description: Minneapolis : Lerner Publications , [2022] | Series: Epic sports bios (Lerner sports) | Includes bibliographical references and index. | Audience: Ages 7–11 | Audience: Grades 2–3 | Summary: "Hank Aaron hit the ball like few other baseball players could. His 755 career home runs rank second on MLB's all-time list. Learn about his journey from the Negro Leagues to the MLB record books"— Provided by publisher.
Identifiers: LCCN 2020048958 (print) | LCCN 2020048959 (ebook) | ISBN 9781728404295 (library binding) | ISBN 9781728420479 (paperback) | ISBN 9781728418070 (ebook)
Subjects: LCSH: Aaron, Hank, 1934—-Juvenile literature. | Baseball players—United States—Biography—Juvenile literature.
Classification: LCC GV865.A25 L44 2022 (print) | LCC GV865.A25 (ebook) | DDC 796.357092 [B]—dc23

LC record available at https://lccn.loc.gov/2020048958
LC ebook record available at https://lccn.loc.gov/2020048959

Manufactured in the United States of America
1-48487-49001-2/2/2021

TABLE OF CONTENTS

BEYOND BABE

On April 8, 1974, one of baseball's greatest records was about to fall as the Atlanta Braves faced the Los Angeles Dodgers. Hank Aaron, Atlanta's star outfielder, needed one home run to pass Babe Ruth's career record of 714. The 53,775 fans at Georgia's Atlanta Stadium buzzed with excitement.

Aaron watches the ball fly against the Dodgers.

FACTS AT A GLANCE

Date of birth: February 5, 1934

Positions: right field and first base

Leagues: Negro Leagues and Major League Baseball (MLB)

Professional highlights: broke Babe Ruth's career home run record; hit 755 career home runs; elected to the National Baseball Hall of Fame in 1982

Personal highlights: grew up in Mobile, Alabama; played fast-pitch softball in high school; nicknamed Hammerin' Hank

Hammerin' Hank came to bat in the fourth inning. The waist-high pitch was just what he wanted to see. Aaron slugged the ball toward deep left-center field. It soared over the fence and bounced into the Atlanta bullpen.

Aaron had just become baseball's new home run king. He had done what once seemed impossible—he'd hit 715 home runs. The crowd erupted in loud cheers. After he rounded the bases, his parents hugged him.

Some of Aaron's teammates wait for him at home plate to celebrate the record-breaking homer.

Aaron's 715th home run ball is on display at the National Baseball Hall of Fame in Cooperstown, New York.

Aaron reflected on his achievement. "At that moment, I knew what the past twenty-five years of my life had all been about," he said. "I had done something that nobody else in the world had ever done." Every home run he hit after this point would set a new record—one that belonged to him.

DREAMING BIG

Henry Louis Aaron was born on February 5, 1934, in Mobile, Alabama. He was the third child of Herbert and Estella Aaron. Hank found time to play baseball whenever he could.

Hank's high school, Central High, didn't have a baseball team. At the time, Alabama schools were segregated. Only schools for white students had baseball teams.

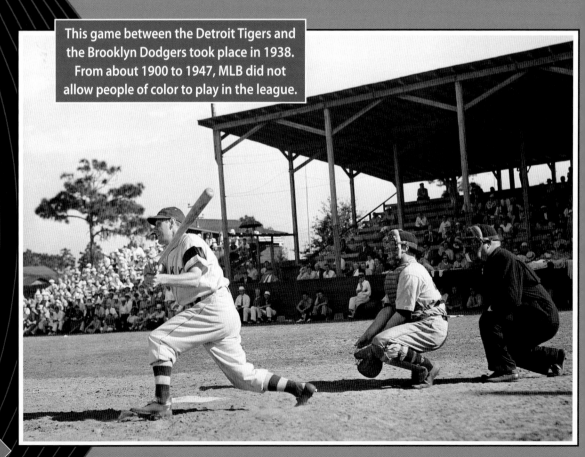

This game between the Detroit Tigers and the Brooklyn Dodgers took place in 1938. From about 1900 to 1947, MLB did not allow people of color to play in the league.

Jackie Robinson played in 10 MLB seasons and helped the Brooklyn Dodgers win the 1955 World Series.

Hank dreamed of playing in MLB. But his father told him that Black people weren't allowed to play in the league. African Americans and other people of color who wanted to play pro baseball had to join the Negro Leagues. Then, in 1947, Jackie Robinson broke the MLB color barrier. He joined the Brooklyn Dodgers to become the first African American major leaguer.

Hank played on Central High's fast-pitch softball team. He played several positions, including catcher and pitcher. And he hit a good number of home runs.

Hank's baseball talent was obvious, but he also played football. His mother was upset when he quit football in high school to focus on baseball. She'd hoped Hank could earn a college scholarship as a football player.

In 1952, 18-year-old Aaron left high school. He joined the Indianapolis Clowns of the Negro Leagues. The young shortstop batted .400 and helped the Clowns win game after game. MLB teams sent scouts to watch Aaron play.

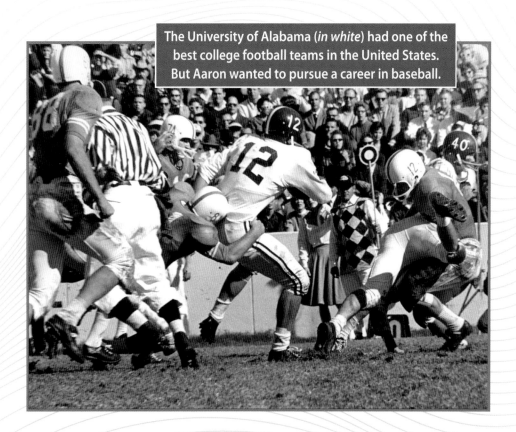

The University of Alabama (*in white*) had one of the best college football teams in the United States. But Aaron wanted to pursue a career in baseball.

Boston Braves general manager John Quinn (*right*) signed Aaron to a contract in 1952. Quinn said it was the best move of his career.

Suddenly, several teams were interested in Aaron. A bidding war broke out between the Brooklyn Dodgers and the Boston Braves. The New York Giants wanted him too. Aaron decided to go with the Braves. They offered him $350 a month, $100 more than the Giants did. But Aaron wouldn't play in the major leagues right away. He'd have to prove himself in other leagues first.

In 1953, Aaron joined the Puerto Rican League. After seeing his strong throwing arm, Aaron's new coaches moved him to the outfield. He finished the season third in the league in batting average (.322) and tied for first in home runs (9). He even won the Most Valuable Player (MVP) award in the league All-Star Game. Aaron was ready for MLB.

Aaron makes a catch in the outfield.

MAKING HIS MARK

In the spring of 1954, Aaron joined the Braves' major-league team. The team had moved to Milwaukee, Wisconsin, the year before. On April 23, he slugged his first major-league home run. By the end of the season, he had hit 12 more. "Once I got [comfortable], I found that playing in the big leagues wasn't nearly as hard as getting there," Aaron said.

Aaron posed for this photo at Ebbets Field in Brooklyn, New York, in 1954.

In 1955, Aaron made the game look easy. A hot first half of the season earned him his first trip to the MLB All-Star Game. By season's end, he'd batted .314, hit 27 homers, had 106 RBIs, and was named the team's MVP.

Aaron kept getting better. On September 24, 1957, he banged out his 44th home run of the season. The blast secured his first National League (NL) home run title. He also led the league with 132 RBIs. The Braves won the NL title and faced the New York Yankees in the World Series.

HAMMERIN' HANK

During the 1955 season, Aaron earned a new nickname—Hammerin' Hank. A New York sportswriter used the name in a newspaper story about one of Aaron's home runs. The Braves' traveling secretary, Donald Davidson, liked the sound of it. He convinced others to start using the nickname.

Aaron takes a practice swing before stepping to home plate.

The Yankees were the clear favorites. They had already won 17 world championships. The Braves—back when they were still in Boston—had won just one. But Aaron and his crew refused to back down from New York's superstars.

New York won the first game 3–1. Aaron energized his team in Game 2 by hitting a triple. The Braves won 4–2. But back in Milwaukee for Game 3, despite a homer by Aaron, the Braves fell apart. They lost 12–3.

In Game 4, Aaron smacked a three-run homer in the bottom of the fourth inning. With the Braves leading 4–1 at the end of the eighth, a win seemed certain. But with two runners on base, Elston Howard—the first African American Yankees player—smacked a home run and tied the game. The Braves finally won 7–5 in the 10th inning. "After that, we felt like we couldn't be beaten," said Aaron.

Aaron hits a three-run homer in Game 4 of the World Series. The blast gave the Braves a 3–0 lead.

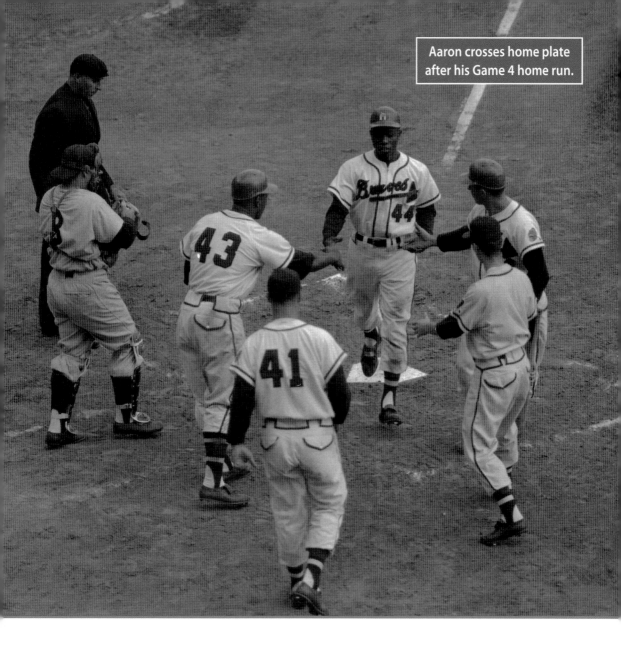

Aaron crosses home plate after his Game 4 home run.

The Braves took Game 5, 1–0. In Game 6, Aaron hit his third World Series home run, but New York won 3–2. Game 7 was all about the Braves. Milwaukee won 5–0. Aaron and the Braves were officially the best in baseball.

MR. 3,000

In 1958, Aaron and the Braves were eager for another trip to the World Series. Milwaukee became NL champions for the second year in a row. Aaron finished with a .326 average, 30 home runs, and 95 RBIs.

In the World Series, the Braves met up with the Yankees for the second straight year. Milwaukee won three of the first four games. But the Yankees came back to win the final three games.

Aaron prepares to make a catch during Game 4 of the 1958 World Series.

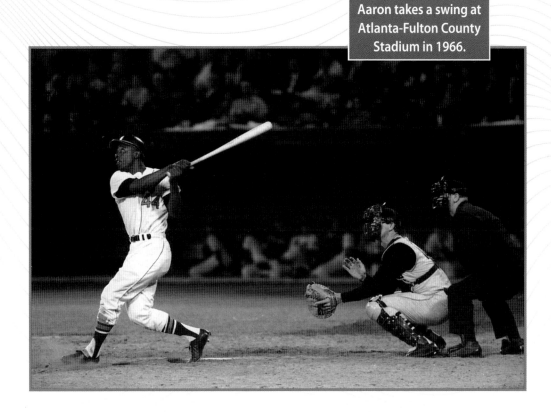

Aaron takes a swing at Atlanta-Fulton County Stadium in 1966.

The early 1960s were tough for the Braves. In 1964, rumors spread that the team would move to Atlanta, Georgia. Although Aaron had a .328 average and 24 home runs, the Braves were in a major slump. They finished in fifth place. On September 20, 1965, Aaron hit his 398th career homer, the last ever hit by a Milwaukee Braves player in Milwaukee. The team moved to Atlanta after the season.

During the Braves' first home game in Atlanta on April 12, 1966, Aaron didn't hit a home run. But by season's end, he was the NL's top home run hitter (44) for the third time in his career. He also won his fourth RBI crown (127).

Aaron just kept hitting. In July 1969, he rocketed his 537th home run, putting him third on the all-time home run list. On May 17, 1970, he made his 3,000th career hit. The

Aaron hit 44 home runs in a season four times: 1957, 1963, 1966, and 1969

GOLD HAMMER

In Atlanta's 1970 home opener against the San Francisco Giants, Aaron hit the first home run to land in the left-field upper deck of Atlanta-Fulton County Stadium. Afterward, the team painted a gold hammer on the seat to mark the spot where Aaron's homer landed.

3,000-hit club had only eight other members at the time. Aaron was the first African American player to join it.

On April 27, 1971, Aaron hit his 600th homer. He ended the season with 47 blasts, his highest total ever. During the 1972 season, Aaron's batting average was down. But he kept hitting long home runs. On June 10, he hit his 649th homer, moving him past Willie Mays into second place on the all-time list. Aaron was in position to break Ruth's record.

HOME RUN KING

After the 1972 season, Aaron hosted a bowling tournament to raise money for sickle cell anemia research. Sickle cell anemia is a disease that mostly affects people of African descent. Aaron pulled together an all-star guest list of sports superstars. "It made me proud to think that I could attract all those great people and made me feel good to see them giving up their time for a worthy cause," Aaron said.

Some of MLB's biggest stars played in Aaron's bowling tournament, including Reggie Jackson and Tom Seaver.

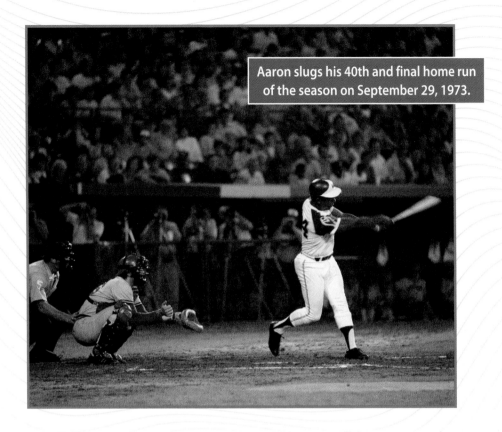
Aaron slugs his 40th and final home run of the season on September 29, 1973.

Going into the 1973 season, Aaron was only 41 homers away from reaching Babe Ruth's record. Aaron's 700th homer came in a game on July 21. With all the excitement, he was constantly surrounded by the media. He received letters from supporters as well as hate mail from people who didn't want him to break Ruth's record. In 1973, Aaron received 930,000 letters, more than any other US citizen. On September 29, the next-to-last day of the season, he increased his home run total to 713.

On April 4, 1974, 40-year-old Aaron arrived at Cincinnati's Riverfront Stadium to face the Reds. In the first inning, he whacked a homer into the left-center-field seats. He had done it—he had tied Babe Ruth's record! Hank ran around the bases with tears in his eyes.

Aaron clubbed his 714th career home run with his first swing of the 1974 season.

Aaron's 715th career home run helped the Braves beat the Dodgers 7–4.

On April 8, back on his home turf, Aaron was ready. It was the season opener in Atlanta, and fans filled the seats to see Aaron break Ruth's record. During the fourth inning, his 715th home run sailed into baseball history.

Aaron was the new home run king. More than 35 million TV viewers and radio listeners had experienced the moment. Aaron's achievement made news around the world.

Aaron spent the final two seasons of his career with the Milwaukee Brewers. On October 3, 1976, he played in his final major-league game. He ended his career with 755 home runs.

Aaron warms up before batting in 1975.

Aaron talks to Tommy Lasorda before an old-timers game in Los Angeles, California, in August 1982. Lasorda managed the Dodgers from 1976 to 1996.

On August 1, 1982, Aaron joined the Baseball Hall of Fame. He died in January 2021. Aaron will always be linked to the sport he loves. "It's the means I have to make a little difference in the world," he said.

SIGNIFICANT STATS

Career home runs: 755, second in MLB history behind Barry Bonds (762)

Career runs batted in: 2,297, the most in MLB history

Led the NL in runs scored: 3 times

Won the 1957 NL MVP award

Was voted to play in the MLB All-Star Game: 25 times

GLOSSARY

blast: a home run

bullpen: a place on a baseball field where pitchers warm up before they start pitching

Negro Leagues: former baseball leagues that were made up of African Americans and other people of color

pro: short for professional, taking part in an activity to make money

RBI: a run in baseball that is driven in by a batter

scholarship: money that a school or another organization gives to students to help pay for their education

segregated: organized to keep members of different races apart, either by dividing facilities into different sections or creating separate facilities for members of certain races

shortstop: the player who defends the infield area on the third-base side of second base

triple: a base hit that allows the batter to reach third base safely

SOURCE NOTES

7 Hank Aaron, *I Had a Hammer: The Hank Aaron Story*, with Lonnie Wheeler (New York: HarperCollins, 1991), 373.

13 Aaron, 122.

16 Aaron, 177.

22 Aaron, 306.

27 Aaron, 456.

LEARN MORE

Fishman, Jon M. *Baseball's G.O.A.T.: Babe Ruth, Mike Trout, and More*. Minneapolis: Lerner Publications, 2020.

Flynn, Brendan. *Atlanta Braves All-Time Greats*. Mendota Heights, MN: Press Box Books, 2021.

Hank Aaron: National Baseball Hall of Fame https://baseballhall.org/hall-of-famers/aaron-hank

Harris, Duchess, and Alex Kies. *The Negro Leagues*. Minneapolis: Core Library, 2020.

Kelly, Matt. "Timeline of Hammerin' Hank's Legendary Career." Major League Baseball, February 5, 2020. https:// www.mlb.com /news/featured/hank-aaron-career-timeline.

Negro Leagues Baseball Museum https://nlbm.com

INDEX

PHOTO ACKNOWLEDGMENTS

Image credits: AP Photo//Harry Harrris, p. 4; Todd Strand/Independent Picture Service, pp. 5, 28; AP Photo/SEBO, p. 6; AP Photo/BOB DAUGHERTY, p. 7; AP Photo, pp. 8, 11, 13, 16, 24; AP Photo/JOHN ROONEY, p. 9; AP Photo/Jim Cox/Houston Chronicle, p. 11; AP Photo/Harry L. Hall, p. 12; Everett Collection Historica/Alamy Stock Photo, p. 15; Bettmann/Getty Images, pp. 17, 18; AP Photo/Marion Crowe, p. 19; Focus on Sport// Getty Images, p. 20; Creative Stock Studio/Shutterstock.com, p. 22; AP Photo/Charles Kelly, p. 23; AP Photo/Charles Pugh, p. 25; AP Photo/Paul Shane, p. 26; AP Photo/Craig Molenhouse, p. 27.

Cover: Louis Requena/MLB/Getty Images; Bettmann/Getty Images.